Frank Kleinholz: A Self Portrait

FRANK KLEINHOLZ:

A SELF PORTRAIT

Introduction by Philip Evergood

SHOREWOOD PUBLISHERS INC., NEW YORK

To Sherry, Jerry, Wendy, Patty & Richard and any others in the making — Love, Frank Kleinholz 4/5/64

TO

Lidia   Lisa   Marco   Anna

CONTENTS

In today's world of Art where gore flows so readily, where at least 50 per cent of the best talents of this day seem to be vying with each other vivisectionally for such honors as "Graphic dismemberer supreme" or "grand inquisitor of internal anatomy" or just plain exerting every muscle, nerve and fibre of their beings to out-horroring Goya in his everlasting humane and powerful exposures of man's cruelty to man, we find Frank Kleinholz plying his gentler craft. This is the expression of simpler little facts of life such as LOVE, Children, Mothers, Babies, Backyards, Swings, Rooftops—A Tree in Brooklyn or a Telegraph Pole in Port Washington—even perhaps a picnic in Central Park.

Kleinholz is a tranquil man in mind and habits. Believing in Peace, non-violence and family living, his work reflects his way of life and his ideology in a gentle yet positive manner. There is nothing especially strong in aspiring to the expression of violence either by the portrayal of ugliness, disintegration, decay or in the assertion of the scene of man's uncertain position in the Universe by continually stressing his charred and broken limbs and mutilated corpse.

Being positive, direct and hopeful is more art-worthy. The most powerful works of art already done, have clearly been made as monuments to the beauty of Man's form and mind which confirm his powers of tenacity for survival under the chaotic and uncertain conditions which Man's unpredictable nature so often imposes and which Nature continually imposes.

Great power and strength has been given to the portrayal of things sweet and tender in the immortal works of Leonardo, Rodin, Renoir, Albert Pinkham Ryder, Giotto and a host of others, why not today search for an interesting way—a new way to show Man unsevered, unbroken—a UNIFIED shape like a pear or an apple of Cézanne?

It is much easier to play with fragments (such as bits of a femur bone, a split pelvis and a horrifying spilling of the contents of an abdominal cavity) and come up with a momentarily spectacular interplay of forms, colors, textures, etc., than to build something complete, whole, lasting, understandable and humane like Cranach's *Eve*, Beckmann's *Fisherwomen* or Van Gogh's little old *Bedroom Chair*. Some of you at this point will be saying—"So who is this Evergood to be talking about temperate climates? He who painted *An American Tragedy,* the scene on a bloody strife-torn heath during a labor battle in Gary, Indiana; he who dealt with nuclear-minded mankind in *Strange Bird Contemplating the Doom of Man, Holocaust* and many another explosive statement in paint? This Evergood, who may possibly have influenced and even given incentive to some of these younger graphic butchers of today who depict nightmares out of their pessimisms, doubts, and fears." If this is what you're saying I must point out that I have dealt with many phases of life from the atrocious and ridiculous to the gentle and sublime and even to the pretty. A sweet taste of sugar, from time to time I'm never ashamed to take in a world where things are constantly so bitter—in ART it can be a welcome relief if it is not overindulged in to the point of sickly sentimentality. The old masters and the young masters all understood this. For all my fears and hatred of oppression I never allowed myself to become morbid, and I have always tried to avoid repetitions and limited clichés. I search for Truth, but I have Hope.

I set myself early to rubbing shoulders with simple people during the past half century or so and I learned that the mass of people are those who ultimately judge an artist, an author, a playwright or a poet. The common people are the ones to be reckoned with ultimately and I have listened to their opinions and their comments. Under a very slow process of grinding and sifting, the true, the purposeful, the potent remains for them in all its clarity and distinction. That is what posterity means in the limited time element of this limited expression of the limitations and beauties and powers of the Human Race.

Frank Kleinholz has in his work a directness, an innocence which is refreshing in today's world of the split atom. His subjects are chosen by a fanciful poetic nature which seeks to get enjoyment in simple and happy things.

Frank's life is a simile of the Gauguin tradition. I won't say he is a product or a copy of it, for he never shut himself away on a "desert island." He has always lived in the struggle and turmoil of big city life. A well-established lawyer in his own right, he had to wait until his forties to accept himself as an artist and, later, wait to be accepted as one dedicating his entire life to his art. This has been surely and well established today.

As a painter I think Frank has an affinity to Jerome Myers, Arnold Friedman and also the early work of Sloan, Wilson, Bellows and Henri. When I say this, I'm not particularly involved with material, method or technique but perhaps with his over-all approach to people, animals, streets—a way of seeing things unpretentiously, modestly. I am not referring especially to the candid, the delicate almost winsome quality of his work but definitely to a painterly attitude to LITTLE PEOPLE and to his natural gifts for the use of paint itself. It would be foolish if I endeavored to step into the role of critic here and attempted to discuss the artistic merits of such favorites of mine as *Bravadoes* and *Back Street* from Frank's brush. The paintings speak for themselves in their warmth, humor, and tender searching.

An artist should be seen and not heard when his own work is being judged, but here I am trying to clarify some issues which are important to me and, I believe, universal as well.

Frank Kleinholz is my friend. Someone I respect and love, but more than that he is an Artist trying to express Life and Society—important values. The key to it all is a fervent love of People.

Frank Kleinholz: A Self Portrait

I should have known better. I should have known better when Sam Shore, the publisher, suggested that I write my own story—a profile, a self portrait. My own words, he said, no matter how simple and crude would be of more interest than the usual introduction that graces most books about artists. I should have known better and said "no." If I had, I would not now be plagued by images and words that I thought I had put to bed long ago. It is so easy to talk and, for me, so much easier to paint.

In my youth I fancied myself a poet. Walking my blind father around the streets of Williamsburg—Humboldt to Meserole to Graham to Montrose Avenue and back to Humboldt Street, we repeated this sequence of four blocks over and over, weather notwithstanding. I walked with him for over sixteen years. I got to know those few streets in and out; every building façade, every bit of pavement, every face in every window, the people in the neighborhood, the hangers-on at the street corners. My father loved this walk, and loved to talk. I listened—a small boy leading a blind man. I asked him what he could see. He told me he could see everything—in his mind. I often played blind and walked in dark rooms, halls and alleyways to see if I could find my way in the dark. My blind father could; I who could see, could not. I marveled at his ability to light his pipe, to get about the house without help, to do small chores.

As we walked he talked of the fields, of his village in Bucovina, of the dibbuks—the ghosts, a world of fantasy made alive by his belief in their reality. He talked of his work in the old country, his father, brothers, sisters. How he came to America, why he came and why he settled in Brooklyn—in Williamsburg. He talked of my mother, Bessie—how he met her in a sweat-shop in Williamsburg, their love and their marriage. He talked of his ambitions for me and counseled me "Learn! Learn! Get an education." Suddenly he stopped and touched my face with sensitive caressing fingers. "You are growing up to be a nice boy," he said. I knew he saw with his fingers.

Some day I thought I would put those words of his down and make them mine, alive and living. But I never did. I tried, tried desperately, but I never did for they were not my words, and in the long run, it was my voice, my own words that I was searching for.

I wrote, and like many a young man, fancied myself a poet. I discovered that poets loved and wrote about their loves—a pleasant way to play with words. I tried it. Some of the poems made the columns of *The New York Globe, The Call* and *The Tribune.* They are all dust now. Among all the papers I have accumulated through the years I cannot find a copy. But I remember some of the girls I wrote about; Matia, Mary, Sylvia, among others. Matia—a name made for poetry. She lived in the rear house, top floor, on Humboldt Street. Italian, newly-arrived in this country. Dark, beautiful, silent. In no time they had her working in a clothing factory. Her delicate, rosy cheeks did not last long in Williamsburg. I remember the lines of a popular Jewish song; "Die Beckelech Vie Rota Pomerantzen—Hoben sich Schoen ausgegreent Ingansen." TB, and Matia was no more. Sentimental? Not to Matia.

There were hallways and roofs, summer in the streets, ventures to Newton Creek, Coney Island, lessons in love and sex-talk on street corners. Gangs, for the young and old, hangouts, drug addicts, whores, gangsters, killings on street corners, life lived in the streets, out in the open for all to see and share. This was the soil that would nurture many writers. This was 1910 to 1920, the period before and after World War I. This was the time when we all were dreaming of writing the Great American Novel. In a way, we all followed a similar pattern.

My parents were Jewish. My mother, Bessie, came from Minsk, Russia; my father, Hyman, from Bucovina, Rumania. They met here and married. I was born on McKibben Street in Williamsburg, Brooklyn, on February 17, 1901; my sister Ruth some five years later. We graduated from public school and went to work soon after graduation. If we wanted a further education, we got it by going to night school. There was a fever sweeping through Williamsburg and other places in the land, a fever of creativity—of wanting to do something, say something, make something out of our days and nights, something we couldn't define.

I ate up books. I couldn't read them fast enough. Later, I read my way through the Colby College Library, indiscriminate reading—one shelf after another. I discovered some interesting writers that way.

With the first money I earned I bought books, mostly poets—Keats, Shelley, Byron and Burns. ("Learn! Learn!") I couldn't wait for my teachers to teach me. Besides I didn't trust them or their ability to teach me. I read and re-read. I recited poetry to anyone who would listen. Prospect Park on a Sunday, the Palisades; and, in the twenties, I discovered Union City over in New Jersey. I discovered food and drink, Sylvia and Ralph Shapiro and their friends, and walks down the streets of Union City to the Hudson River to see the sun rise over the New York City skyscrapers. Through Sylvia and Ralph I met people interested in writing and in the theatre; Moss Hart, Dore Schary, and many others. I learned that the fever was sweeping Union City and Newark too. Now I was certain I was going to be a writer. I let my hair grow long and bought a cane.

I have often wondered who threw the switch and made me choose the law as a profession. I remember my bar mitzvah. It is customary at bar mitzvahs for the young man to make a speech. My rabbi, like others, had a book of speeches for these occasions, and I had to memorize one that he chose. From the platform in front of the Ark in the Synagogue on McKibben Street, I recited the speech. Later that night celebrating at home with friends and relatives, my Uncle Lovejoy, loaded with wine, made me recite the speech over again—not once, but three times. He just loved it. In his pompous way he announced to my father: "Hyman, that boy has got to be a lawyer!" Whether he planted the seed or not doesn't matter now. I think I chose the law for the simple reasons that the tuition was cheapest, the course easiest and I could work in the daytime and attend school at night—all economic and, for me and my parents, compelling reasons.

I had to bring some dollars home to help my parents. My father being blind, did no work. My mother ran a candy and delicatessen store, took care of the home, took care of my father and his two children by a former marriage, cooked meals for us and for some of the laborers who worked in the neighborhood, took in all the relatives who were coming to the Golden Land, America, from Europe and housed and fed them until they made roots here, observed the Sabbath, kept a kosher home, instilled the fear of God in us, served us, washed us, dressed us and suffered from migraine headaches. My mother is still alive, alert and wise at ninety. I often ask her, "How did you do it?" She smiles her tragic smile and answers, "How did I do it? I did it."

I did it. I sold Jewish newspapers with my friend Joe Battaglia on the corner of Varet and Graham Avenues. It was during the war, and Joe could yell; "Premyzl hat geffallen" as well as I could. Public school was all they could carry me through. A graduation ring, a blue serge suit, a white flower in my buttonhole, an afternoon at Fox's Folly, and I was launched into the world, ready at fourteen, armed with "working papers". I was "a man" —as the comics jokingly referred to the standard cliché of the bar mitzvah speech: A man with a job bringing home three or four dollars a week, going to Eastern District High School at night ("Learn! Learn!").

What a life. It doesn't even look good in retrospect. There was no romance or glory in getting up mornings in a cold, unheated flat in the dead of winter, taking a trolley car to New York and chasing myself around Bleecker and West Broadway delivering boxes of caps (carrying them—we had no carts) from dealer to dealer for three dollars a week. On Mondays I came in at seven a.m. to sweep out the shop. It didn't take me too long to realize that this might have been what was good for Horatio Alger—but not for me.

I found another job in a drugstore on Manhattan Avenue within walking distance of my home and although the salary was no higher, the atmosphere was more intellectual and sweeping out a drugstore more dignified. Besides, Boris, the pharmacist, was an intellectual who sat in a Morris chair in back of the store all day reading the books he sent me to the Public Library for. Good books too. Thanks to Boris, I learned of Balzac, Turgenev, Tolstoi, G. B. Shaw, Marx, Victor Hugo and many, many other great writers and thinkers. I read them all. Some I understood, some not. But something always stuck.

Among Boris, night school and the streets of Williamsburg, I was getting a well-rounded education. There were street-corner meetings at Graham and Varet Streets held by groups of every shade and degree of opinion where I got my first lessons in economics. I met fellows who had been beaten up on picket lines and who in turn had beaten up scabs. I met religionists, atheists, all who wanted to convert me. I bought their literature and read it and learned about Eugene V. Debs, Robert Ingersoll, Bill Foster. I read the *Liberator,* later called the *Masses,* and learned about Max Eastman, Dreiser, Floyd Dell and Art Young. I sent some poems to the *Masses* and they were rejected, the rejection slips reading "Sorry—Try Again. M. G.". I knew all about rejection slips and received my share of them.

The evening classes at Eastern District High School were a bore. It would take me eight years of night study to graduate. When I learned of "Prep" schools and Regents' exams I started going to Eron Prep School on the East Side of New York and then to the Bedford YMCA in Brooklyn. One of my teachers, Mr. Colcord, told me that he could get me a work scholarship at Colby College in Waterville, Maine, that would take care of my tuition and most of my living costs. I decided to go to Colby.

Of course, I had to talk it over with my mother and father. Working as a page in the New York Cotton Exchange at the time I was earning fair money, most of which went home. My mother told me she had saved some money from my salary. They could spare me for the school year. The day came, I packed my belongings in a cardboard valise, they walked me to Graham Avenue where I took a trolley to New York. My mother, stocky, wearing a bulky sweater, my father gray and dignified. They stood there and waved good-by. My first good-by.

As I stood there I talked to Mrs. Battaglia, Joe's mother. "Mrs. Battaglia," I said, "I am going to college." I talked to the Russos, the Feinbergs who lived on Montrose Avenue and to Mr. Amato who had the grocery store next door, to all my pals who hung out at the candy stand at Meserole Street and of course to all my relatives, some of whom were even rich. I particularly wanted the rich ones to know that Frank Kleinholz, the son of Bessie and Hyman Kleinholz, was going to college.

I have never wanted to go back to revisit Colby College. I didn't want to go back because I knew it could never be as beautiful as I remembered it. It wasn't much of a place then, certainly not by today's standards. Nothing like it is now with its new campus, new buildings, and several thousand students. It was a small place situated across from the railroad station. There were about 600 students, both boys and girls. The tuition was low, and most of the students were on part or full scholarships. I arrived in Waterville at night and slept at the YMCA near the station. A mighty homesick night. In the morning I saw Colby. I was going to college. A miracle of sorts.

This was a new world to me. The people were different from any I had known. They were almost all Christians. There were only six Jewish students at the school. I had known Christians before, but these were different. Quite different from my Italian and Irish neighbors at home. They were quiet, decorous and had no foreign accents. Their foods were different; their manners and talk different. They were strange to me, almost too kind and polite. At first I was self-conscious in their presence, but they befriended me and invited me to church on Sunday, (Colby was and is a Baptist college) and to the Christian Endeavor Society meetings. I went, met the young ladies there, danced with them and some of the Williamsburg toughness and hardness began to wear off. Not all of it. I had to be different and exaggerate my "differences". I went in for boxing; it was one of the few talents I had brought from Brooklyn. I did pretty well, but I quit when I noticed my nose changing character. Boxing, I decided, was no profession for me. I studied my new friends and aped their ways and manners. They were all interesting, the girls more so. They seemed so remote, so untouchable, but I soon learned you could make passes at girls who belonged to the Christian Endeavor Society.

I was tending furnace in Hedman Hall for my work scholarship. It was a good job, shoveling coal into the jaws of an ancient furnace. I felt like Yank in O'Neill's *Hairy Ape*. All went well until I asked a friend to take care of the furnace and he forgot. When I returned, the furnace was almost out. In my panic I opened the water valves, filled the hot boiler with cold water and the boiler cracked. There were no excuses, I lost my job. But by this time I knew my way around Waterville, and I soon had two other jobs; one Saturday night selling clothes in a men's shop; the other, Wednesday night teaching two fellow students, both potato farmers, how to fox trot. Tending furnace was easier.

I was looking ahead. This beautiful year would soon end and, much as I wanted to get my degree at Colby, I knew I couldn't stay. The letters from home had a note of urgency. I applied for and received a law-student's qualifying certificate from the New York State Board of Regents. I had continued writing while at Colby. I told myself that I could write while going to law school and when I had become a lawyer. The law would be a life-preserver to keep me afloat as a writer. The life-preserver almost drowned me.

I left Colby, my things packed in the same cardboard suitcase. Leonard Mayo and Chick Gale, two friends who had nurtured me through my first year, taught me the social graces and some etiquette, saw me to the train. As I was boarding the train, the old suitcase gave up and came apart at the seams. It was funny enough to make Chick and Len laugh. I picked up my things and, with the help of Len and Chick, tied up the valise. I left Colby still feeling self-conscious and out of place.

Fordham Law School was in the Woolworth Building on Lower Broadway in Manhattan. I enrolled in the afternoon class and found a job as an office boy in a nearby law office and found some time to write. *The New York Globe* published a vignette I had written about downtown Brooklyn. Later I won first honorable mention in S. Jay Kauf-man's column in the same paper with the poem *Matia*. Eugene Jolas won first prize. I was reading Walt Whitman at the time and started walking the Brooklyn Bridge. It was good exercise, and I walked not only Brooklyn Bridge but Williamsburg Bridge. I soon made it a habit to walk over the Williamsburg Bridge, through Brooklyn, to my home on Humboldt Street. It was not only Whitman who inspired the walk, but I had become body-conscious and wanted to have muscles like Bernarr Macfadden. I read his maga-zine, *Physical Culture,* took weight-lifting exercises and "chewed" milk. He said you had to chew *all* foods, even liquids. I tried to get my friend Joe on this kick, but he liked spaghetti too much. Besides he was going to medical school and had no time for fads. We walked the Williamsburg Bridge together on Sundays, talking about life, our plans, my poems, his studies. Later I painted *The Bridge* which was exhibited at the Carnegie Institute Annual. Joe bought the painting long after he had become a doctor. I also painted *Sunday on the Bridge* which is now in the Sackler Collections.

A psychoanalyst friend who visited me at my studio during the period when I was painting these pictures told me that bridges were "phallic symbols". When I was paint-ing kids climbing poles, he told me that poles, all poles, were "phallic symbols". Later when I was painting trees, he told me that trees were "phallic symbols". One day I told him that he was a big "phallic symbol" and to stop bothering me. Poor fellow. He had lots of money and wanted to buy one of my paintings but couldn't because they were all full of "phallic symbols".

Joe and I traveled to Newark, spending all the time we could spare visiting Sylvia and Ralph Shapiro. They were surrounded by a group of young actors, embryo play-wrights and aspiring writers. This was the world I wanted to live in. There were attrac-tive girls in the circle, and I fell in and out of love, avoiding marriage as a trap until I fell in love and got married. Leah Schwartz was her name. She taught school in the Bronx and lived on East Tremont Avenue. It was rugged taking her home to the Bronx and then travelling all the way home to Brooklyn. One rainy night her mother invited me to stay over, to save me the long trip home in the rain, she said. Six months later we were married. Some years after my sister was seeing a young man who lived out on Long Island. One rainy night I suggested he sleep over. He did. Six months later they were married. Apparently, it works all the time.

There we were, the young school teacher and the young lawyer. I introduced her to my friends in Newark. She knew about my poems and my writing. She also knew that I was a lawyer and needed clients. She introduced me to contract bridge and golf, helped me entertain clients and showed me the comforts of middle-class life. We set up house-keeping in an apartment on Ocean Avenue in Flatbush. There we entertained, played bridge, talked bridge and played more bridge. For relief, we played golf. In the back of my mind there was a faint remembrance of literature. As soon as I had time, I was going to start writing again. But there never seemed to be any time.

When we were very young, my mother took us to Coney Island for a holiday. She took my sister Ruth, Jake, Fanny, and myself. She gave us each a five-cent piece for "spending money". "When you get to Coney Island," she said, "spend it on anything you like." It was a hot, sticky day and a relief to get away from the pavements of Williamsburg. We arrived in Coney Island and what a beautiful sight. What delicious smells, clean skies, peanuts roasting, taffy candy, merry-go-round calliopes playing and a whiff of salt in the air. We looked at everything and wanted to buy everything. Ruthie wanted to buy some spun candy. Save your money for something special.

The Bowery in Coney Island is a short narrow street that leads to the beach. Side shows line both sides of the street, and we stopped in front of one where three girls in semi-transparent silk folds were doing a diminished hootchy-cootchy. The barker kept shouting: "This is the House of Mirrors—Come in—Try to get out—Ten cents for adults —Five cents for children." We were gawking open-mouthed at the show when Ruthie leaped toward the ticket seller and bought a ticket. We tried to stop her, but my mother said, "It's her nickel, let her go". She went in and we waited and waited. Suddenly her face appeared in the small opening of the tent and she cried out, "Help, I'm lost—get me out!" With that, she disappeared. My mother went up to the barker; "Mister, my little girl is inside and can't get out. She's lost. Can I go in and get her?" " Lady," he said, "this is the House of Mirrors. Ten cents for adults. Five cents for children."

My mother looked at me, and I read her mind. I'm not spending my nickel! Jake had to go in. He got lost. Fanny went in. She got lost. She couldn't find Jake or Ruthie and couldn't find her way out. Finally I went in. I got lost. Desperate—my mother went up to the barker again and again he told her: "Sorry, Lady, this is the House of Mirrors. It's ten cents for adults, five cents for children." She finally had to give up a dime to get in, and she got lost. By the time they rounded us up it was late afternoon. There was nothing left to do but go home. My mother didn't say anything, even after we got home. It became a family secret. We were too chagrined to talk about it. Many years later studying for a law exam I was at the kitchen table. My mother was scrubbing clothes in the kitchen sink. I would read a page and then look up at her as she bent over the sink, weary, tired, her hands red in the hot water. She started mumbling something to herself, shaking her head and then stopping suddenly, she straightened out, heaved a sigh and said to nobody in particular, "What a strange country this is! You have to pay to get lost."

"Leah dear," I said, "I am lost; I don't want to play bridge any more. I don't want to fight golf balls. I think I have paid for getting lost, paid with years and with time. I don't know what I want to do. I am certain it isn't writing or I'd still be at it." She said, "Why not take piano lessons?" Her suggestion appealed to me, so I bought a piano, took lessons, and after a year I could play Chopin's *Etude in A Minor, arranged for beginners.*

Leah took great pride in my accomplishment and every time we had guests she would at the opportune time ask me to play "some Chopin". I would unhesitatingly oblige and play Chopin's *Etude in A Minor, arranged for beginners.* But deep inside of me I knew I never would make Carnegie Hall. And strange as it may seem I desperately wanted to make Carnegie Hall.

Kay Kinzler, a friend of Leah's, was painting at the Art Students League. One day she showed me her paintings. They looked pretty good to me. She suggested that I try to paint. Ben Sackheim, another friend, told me he was studying with Alex Dobkin who had a studio on Madison Avenue at 59th Street, opposite the State Insurance Fund offices where I worked. I saw Alex Dobkin and enrolled in his class. This was the beginning. Alex became my friend, my guide, my teacher. He introduced me to a new world, a world of art. He took me to museums, and I began to look at paintings with new eyes. He told me about paint, paint surfaces, the structure of paintings, and he encouraged me. He told me I was a natural painter.

I took the next step and moved out of Brooklyn, out of Flatbush to an apartment on West 16th Street. At the end of six months, Alex told me to try painting with another teacher, someone whose approach was different from his. He suggested I study with Yasuo Kuniyoshi which I did. This was a fortunate choice. Kuniyoshi was a perceptive teacher, delicate and poetic in his work and able to communicate his ideas to students.

The American Art School, then at 14th Street and now, unfortunately, no longer in existence, announced a competition for a scholarship. I submitted two paintings and won a scholarship. Alex thought that Sol Wilson who was teaching there would be a good teacher for me, that my work was somewhat in his style and had some of the elements of his rich color. I left Kuniyoshi's class and studied with Sol Wilson. At the end of the year, Wilson told me to quit studying, to get a studio and paint.

It was customary for the school faculty to choose several promising students for a solo or joint exhibition in the school galleries. At the end of my year they voted me, and Rose Jacobson, a fellow student, a joint exhibition. I exhibited some 20 paintings, among which was *Sunday in the Park* (page 6). My paintings had been derivative, but this painting had a different quality about it. There was something new in it; a transition. The painting helped me make up my mind, convinced me that I had identity as an artist and that I could say something that was mine. I was not worried about techniques. These could be acquired. The important fact was that I had found my subject matter. I knew what I wanted to paint.

I followed Sol Wilson's advice. George Kleinsinger had a beautiful sky-lighted studio with living quarters at 88 Seventh Avenue South in Greenwich Village. When he went into the Army, he turned the studio over to Leah and me. We moved in.

I had made the full cycle—almost. I was still working with the State Insurance Fund. It had its advantages. I could leave the office, cross the street and be painting within half an hour. It also was located in the heart of New York's art galleries. I could make the round of exhibitions. Besides, it paid a weekly salary. But I wanted to cut all ties. I had no dislike for the law as such, but I had no great liking for it either. The little time I spent at the law was that much time lost at painting. Worse, it split me in two, lawyer and painter. I did not want to think like a lawyer, act like a lawyer. I wanted to purge myself of the law, clients, law books. I wanted to be all painter, all artist.

Life was pushing me along and in 1941, I submitted *Abstractionists* (page 32) to the Carnegie Institute's exhibition "Directions in American Painting". It was a major national exhibition. It was my first submission to any exhibition. My painting *Abstractionists* was accepted and received much critical acclaim. Forbes Watson writing in the *Magazine of Art,* November, 1941, said, among other things, "The picture in the exhibition which most won my affections [is] a painting called *Abstractionists* by Frank Kleinholz. I don't know Mr. Kleinholz, but I imagine that we have in common a great admiration—Max Weber. Does this mean a direction? Toward what? Toward wit, superb color, a very personal sense of design, a natural escape from the obvious."

A year later reviewing my first one-man show, the late Edward Alden Jewell, art critic for the *New York Times* wrote:

"Quite unknown only a little more than a year ago, Mr. Kleinholz was 'discovered' when the jury of selection met to decide what pictures were to be admitted to the 1941 'Directions in American Painting' shown at the Carnegie Institute in Pittsburgh. The roster of that exhibition had been limited to artists who had never before participated in a Carnegie International. Out of nearly 5000 entries, the jury chose 302, among them being a canvas sent by this newcomer, Frank Kleinholz.

The picture was called *Abstractionists*—a street scene with some little boys sketchily drawing diagrams with chalk on wall and side-walk. The simple chalked diagrams, but especially the whole construction of scene, made the title appropriate. It was clever, but it was a great deal more than that. It was a fresh note. It was arresting, alive. I thought it one of the best things in the exhibition."

John O'Connor, Jr., the Acting Director of the Carnegie Institute's Department of Fine Arts, wrote me that several offers had been made for my painting. Would I sell? He submitted an offer, I accepted it, and then told me he was the purchaser.

I had sold a painting! I was no longer an amateur, I no longer considered myself a "Sunday painter", a phrase I intensely disliked. I was a "pro" and like all professionals in every field I wanted to dedicate myself completely to my work. The reception the painting received, the sale to Mr. O'Connor was just the beginning. Reeves Lewenthal of the Associated American Artists Galleries, asked me to join his gallery then at 711

Fifth Avenue, New York City, and scheduled me for a one-man exhibition for December, 1942. I continued to send paintings to juried exhibitions, and *Siesta* (page 34), now in the Joseph H. Hirshhorn collection, was accepted for the Pennsylvania Academy Annual. *Halloween Harlequins,* later purchased by Herman Wechsler of the F.A.R. Gallery, New York, was accepted by the Virginia Museum's Third Biennial. Duncan Phillips invited me to exhibit at the Phillips Gallery of Art in Washington, D.C. Later that year the jury for "Artists for Victory" in its exhibition at the Metropolitan Museum of Art, selected two of my paintings *Back Street* (page 36) and *Bargain Counter* for the exhibition. With the notice of acceptance was a check for $500 and a letter advising me that I had been awarded the sixth purchase prize and that the painting was acquired by the Metropolitan Museum of Art for its permanent collection under the terms of the prize. Among the prize winners were John Steuart Curry, Jack Levine, Marsden Hartley, Alexander Calder, Philip Evergood, Jacob Lawrence, and Mark Tobey. I did not go to work that day.

In December, 1942, I held my first one-man show at the Associated American Artists Galleries. I sold fairly well and received excellent notices. Edward Alden Jewell gave me a feature story in which he wrote that in his opinion "Frank Kleinholz is here to stay". Mr. O'Connor wrote the foreword to my catalogue. I quote it in full:

"I would like to think that I discovered Frank Kleinholz. Nothing would please me better than that honor. I did not discover him, for, paradoxical as it may seem, he discovered himself. He possessed the instincts of an artist and needed only to apply paint in his own inimitable way to canvas to discover himself as a new figure in American art. It is a matter of record that the Jury of Admission for the Carnegie Institute exhibition, 'Directions in American Painting,' selected one hundred and thirty-seven out of some two thousand, two hundred and sixty-four which passed before it one day in New York. If anyone besides himself discovered Frank Kleinholz, the honor is the Jury's.

The characteristic that distinguishes all painting from other forms of art expression is its color. It is 'the without which not' of painting; it is the color that matters. I am well aware that all artists use color, but it is often a minor consideration with them, so much are they occupied with the other elements of their art. It is color, rich, luscious, abundant, subtle in its variations, and revealing, that is Frank Kleinholz's chief concern, and I say he has chosen the better part. He is not afraid of his medium, he glories in it. He puts down what he sees with his mind's eye as spots of rather than forms. His second interest is design which he carries through his paintings in an intriguing manner. To these two elements he adds a very personal approach—the fillip—which gives distinction to his paintings."

Miss Emily Genauer, then art critic for the *New York World Telegram* (now of the *New York Herald Tribune*) coupled my show with that of my good friend David Burliuk under the heading "Burliuk and Kleinholz". *Newsweek* called me "The Brooklyn-Born Gauguin."

I walked down Fifth Avenue and looked up at the windows of the Associated American Artists Galleries. There in the window was one of my paintings and underneath it the sign "Exhibition; Frank Kleinholz".

There were other exhibitions, invitations to national exhibitions that year and in the years that followed. Duncan Phillips invited me to have a one-man exhibition at The Phillips Gallery held in May 1943 and in the same year I was elected a member of the American Group.

The door had opened, in fact, it was wide open. I was 42, a part-time lawyer and part-time artist. There didn't seem to be much time and I had so much painting to do, so many pictures in my mind I wanted to get down on canvas. My wife Leah was teaching school. I was selling and exhibiting, so why not just walk through the door. I wanted to quit the State Insurance Fund and give up the practice of the law.

It was not that simple and not that easy. Leah and I talked about it. She agreed that sooner or later I would have to make the change. She asked me to wait just another year or two. I agreed, and it was fortunate that I did, for within a year she became ill with cancer, an illness which lasted over two years and took all of our resources, all of the money we had both earned and saved. I loved Leah, she was a beautiful woman and a good woman. I never saw her cry or pity herself. Two years of it. In December, 1944, I had my second one-man show at the gallery. She said that she wanted to be at the opening, and she made it. Wasted as she was, she dressed in an evening gown, wore a corsage of flowers, greeted guests and then went back to her bed. She died November 25, 1945.

I was alone—no children, no responsibilities. I handed in my resignation and walked out of the State Insurance Fund. I called Manny Price, my law partner, and told him he could have my law books, office furniture and other paraphernalia and asked him to wind up what little law work I had. I never went back to my law office. I never went back to the State Insurance Fund. I did go to the funerals of a few of my colleagues at the Fund who had planned to work there until they could retire on their pensions.

Burliuk was celebrating one of his birthdays at a little restaurant in Greenwich Village, and I was a guest along with other friends. A young lady was sitting behind me, her back to me. I wanted to see her face. I tapped her on the shoulder and when she turned to look at me, I asked "And who are you?" "Lidia Brestovan." I learned that she was a teacher at the Little Red School House on Bleecker Street. I often saw her walking the children along Seventh Avenue, and I painted her walking her class. I invited her to my studio to see the painting. We were married April 19, 1946.

Life was shaping up the way I wanted it to. I was free of my job, the law. I had all the time to do the thing I thought most important—painting. I wanted to teach painting.

Teaching would clarify my own ideas and improve my techniques. I took on private students, then a few jobs in private schools. The Metropolitan Museum of Art through its Director, the late Francis Henry Taylor, inaugurated art classes for trade union members. He assigned Blanche R. Brown of the Museum to this task and engaged me to conduct classes in sketching and painting.

The State, County and Municipal Workers Union took advantage of this and started classes at their meeting hall. My students were engineers, sanitation workers, truck drivers, stenographers. It was wonderful. I invited Philip Evergood and Harry Gottlieb to give lectures and Blanche Brown lectured on the history of art. I learned that art is not the private preserve of any small group of intellectuals, any special set. These men and women had a great curiosity, a great desire to learn and understand. Contact with them was most rewarding and revealing. I could speak directly to them, I came from the same sources and a year or two ago I had been punching a time clock in an office and was myself a member of the State, County and Municipal Workers Union.

In 1946 I conducted a studio class for the Brooklyn Museum. By this time I felt confident enough to start lecturing. I was offered a chance to conduct a weekly radio series on art over station WNYC in New York. I accepted and interviewed guest artists for over a year and a half. The New York public had an opportunity to become acquainted with the work and lives of American artists.

Reeves Lewenthal was a very imaginative and enterprising dealer; Estelle Mandel, his assistant, a brilliant publicist. Between them, they put the gallery in the front ranks of the galleries of that period. They were always considerate to me, sold my work, arranged exhibitions throughout the United States and handled me and my work with skill and sincerity. I had one-man exhibitions in their galleries in New York, Chicago and Los Angeles. In 1945 *Encyclopaedia Britannica* was collecting a group of paintings by contemporary American artists that was to be formed into a permanent collection and to be called the Encyclopaedia Britannica Collection of Contemporary Art. They purchased my painting *Bravadoes* (page 42), now in the collection of Senator and Mrs. William Benton. Shortly after the purchase I was appointed to the Art Advisory Board of the *Encyclopaedia Britannica*.

Our first child was born on January 2, 1947. She was a beautiful little girl, and we decided to call her Leah after my first wife. We always talked about Leah. It seemed a good idea to have her presence in our home out in the open. It was a romantic notion, but we did not count on the little girl. As soon as she could speak, she changed her name to "Lolly" and later to "Lisa". I had a new role in life, that of father. I began to see and participate in the world of children. I had been painting children before, but not with the understanding I then acquired and developed later. The world of children is a serious world. Children are serious people. They want to be taken seriously. I find them wonderful company, humorous, full of imagination and poetry. I believe most people do not really look at children or listen to them. They should.

It was February, 1948. I had been painting and exhibiting since 1940. I had by this time had about six one-man shows, an invitation to The Phillips Gallery, and my work had been exhibited in almost every important national exhibition.

J. LeRoy Davidson, on behalf of the State Department, had included by purchase, two of my paintings *Bank Night* (page 43) and *White Flowers* (page 47) in the State Department's collection of contemporary art which was to travel to Europe and South America and which did, until stopped by opposition of Congressmen. Included in this collection were works by such outstanding artists as Milton Avery, Ralston Crawford, Stuart Davis, Arthur Dove, Philip Evergood, William Gropper, Marsden Hartley, Kuniyoshi, Jack Levine, John Marin, Georgia O'Keeffe, Abraham Rattner, Anton Refregier, Ben Shahn and others.

I had managed to support myself and partly support my child through the sale of my work. I was considered a great "success." But the real success in art is completely different from success in the business world. If one were to apply one's self to the pursuit of money with all the study, research, time, the dedication an artist puts into his work and career, I am sure he would soon be rich as Croesus. The financial reward for the painter is minimal. Success in art is a success of person, of character, a success of search and discovery. The rewards are far greater than any material reward. That does not mean that there is any virtue in starving or living in a garret. I have yet to meet an artist who thinks so. The only people who think so are well-fed businessmen. Artists need money to live, and they want to live, and, when they can, know how to live sumptuously. They have a natural gift for good living.

I had the kind of success I had always wanted. I had always expected success. When it came, I took it as my due. The lady who interviewed me for *Newsweek* magazine some years before, wrote that I was "not an overly modest man". She was not very perceptive. I had nothing to be modest about. I took my success in the same way I took my failures and my tragedies. They were experiences, the web and skein of life. Failures were incentives and successes were things to forget and from which to run away. I had always felt conscious about my lack of skills. Starting late in life as an artist, I lacked the years of technical training, particularly training in draftsmanship.

There is no substitute, no short cut for years of study and practice, and if I were going to paint life and from life, if I were going to meet the challenges that my ideas entailed, I had to acquire the necessary skills. I decided to go to Paris, to France, to concentrate on drawing for a year. I was helped in my desire by Dr. Arthur Sackler. He came to my studio and bought enough paintings to keep us abroad for at least a year. We sailed in September, 1948.

We were not without friends in Paris. Joseph Floch, a colleague at Associated American Artists, rented his studio on Avenue de Chatillion to me. After a month at the Hotel Lutecia, Lidia swapped an old silver-fox cape her aunt had given her for a flat at 25 Rue Mademoiselle. It consisted of two rooms and kitchen, cold water, no heat, no bath, the toilet in the hall. We found that it had a fireplace that had been boarded over. We opened it and bought a gas heater and a hot-water attachment for the sink. We hung some paintings and prints on the walls, bought a bed, a table, a baby carriage, and we were in business. I had my studio away from home, and Lidia had her home away from me and my clutter.

It was a good time to be in Paris (any old time is a good time to be in Paris). Howard Baer, another gallery artist was there, Sidney Simon, Robert Bigelow, a young American painter and an army of ex-G.I.'s studying under the G.I. Bill. Later Robert Gwathmey, Joseph Hirsch, William Gropper and Paul Strand came over and we had our own group of expatriates. I hired some models, went to the Grand Chaumière where they had life classes at modest fees. I decided to try every avenue where drawing was essential. I tried lithography, etching, woodcuts. I worked with an old lithographer, Dorfinant who had a studio and press in a small street behind Notre Dame. I found a printer of etchings, a fine craftsman who had a complete shop.

Before long I had executed a series of lithographs and etchings which I later took back to New York with me. When I got back, I wanted to check and see how they held up against the work of other etchers and lithographers, and I sent some of them to be juried in open competition. *Boy's Head,* a lithograph, won a purchase prize at Syracuse University. *Ou Est Montparnasse?*, an etching, was exhibited in the 1951 Brooklyn Museum print exhibition, and *Birthday Cake* was exhibited first at the Library of Congress, Washington, D.C. and later that year at Carnegie Institute's "Invitation Exhibition of Prints".

Lidia was discovering Paris. She could speak French and the baby was learning fast. I mastered enough French to find my way around, order food and wine. My limited French vocabulary sufficed me. I would never have a decent accent, My French, delivered with my Brooklyn accent, curled the eyebrows of many a Frenchman. But I didn't go to France to study the language. I went to work and wanted to use all of my time for work. It was too easy to be diverted. There were galleries, cafes to sit at, wines to drink, historic museums to visit and many other delightful temptations. We bought a second hand Peugeot. We would take a week off and travel now and then. To England, Holland, Belgium, and over every bit of France.

We spent one summer on the Isle de Brehat off the coast of Normandy. There was nothing to do there but walk, swim, draw, and drink Normandy cider. Lidia had managed so well that with the few sales I made, we were able to stretch our stay for another year. She also managed on April 1, 1950, to give birth to a baby boy at the American Hospital. We called him Marco Polo and he was a nice souvenir to bring back from Paris.

There is art in every cobblestone, in every street in Paris. The streets are extensions of the museums. There are no harsh changes. Artists paint in the street, in the country-side. They seem to be part of the landscape and part of the life and they can work where they will without drawing a crowd of the curious. We American painters in France discovered the beauty of outdoor painting, of painting directly from life. It was a healthy experience for most of us. It gave us a chance to learn how closely the French Masters had observed the life around them.

Two years slipped by, I was tired of having to rely on a few American friends for talk, gossip, and companionship. I was an alien. No matter how much I loved France, I would never be a part of its life. My stay had been very fruitful, but now it was time to go home, home to the city, home to New York. We sailed late in 1950. Richer by Marco, cases full of paintings, etchings, the wonderful easel I bought in Paris, many more skills and much more knowledge than I had brought to France.

Lidia had lived in Port Washington before our marriage. It is a small town on the North Shore of Long Island facing Manhasset Bay. Many years before, her friend Albert Wood promised her first call if he decided to sell his home. He kept his promise. It was a roomy old house near the waterfront. Our studio in New York had no room for children. There was no play area nearby, no place to keep a baby carriage. We decided to buy Mr. Wood's home. The house had no central-heating system. The heat was supplied by old-fashioned oil stoves which required tending, cleaning and changing of wicks. I remembered my furnace-tending days and refused the responsibility. Lidia assumed it, filling the stoves daily with kerosene, seeing that they were lit and working. Wherever she went she carried a delicate smell of kerosene with her. She started a nursery school in our house. It was immediately sucessful. I converted the carport into a studio where I had a place to work. Every so often she and her students would come into my studio for a visit and chat. I was the foster father of 12 more children. It was a good feeling.

I started some classes, the gallery scheduled me for an exhibition for April, 1951. Something I always wanted came to me at this time—a chance to teach in a college. Hofstra College offered me an instructorship in painting and drawing. I accepted, and again I was on a college campus. This time I didn't talk to Mrs. Battaglia, the fellows at the corner stand or my rich relatives. I spoke to my mother. "Look Ma!" I said, "I'm a Professor!"

My private classes were full, I was teaching at Hofstra College during the day and Adult Education at night. My work was being sold both in and out of the gallery, and now success had come in a material way, but it was encroaching on my painting time. I had an exhibition in Chicago, and a critic, reviewing my exhibition, said that my "color was progressive" but that I shouldn't waste it on painting subject matter. The consensus was that subject matter was out, finished. Abstract art was coming on the scene. Join, or move over and make room. I am not an experimenter trying to find ways to revolutionize art.

I believe that the stream of art throughout the history of man has been concerned principally with man and his place in the world—his relation to his gods, to himself, to his fellow man. In short, with humanity. I believe in clarity as opposed to obscurity; to the plain statement of fact, as opposed to bombast; the resolution of contradictions rather than the exploration of confusions. I want to communicate, to be understood. I paint children, mothers, people in the street, people against buildings, tenements, skyscrapers and a country landscape if it pleases me. As I learn and understand more, my horizons will widen. It has been said that I paint "the little, simple people". I don't believe there are any "little, simple people" any more than there are leprechauns. The so-called "little, simple people" are very complex people.

Through 1952 and 1953 I continued to exhibit, teach and worry about lack of painting time. When things got so bad that I was making more money teaching and selling than I ever did at the law, good fortune helped me out of the dilemma. Hofstra, telling me how much they liked my teaching, failed to rehire me. (But, in 1959, they invited two of my paintings to their "First Annual Invitational Exhibition".) My students dropped off, and soon there was nothing to do but paint.

Bob Bigelow had been writing from Los Angeles where he lived, urging us to come out. It was time for another journey. Another door was opening. Marco was 5, Lolly 8. I bought an Oldsmobile for $300, put new tires on it, a rack on top, filled it with masonite panels, leased our house and in September 1955, set off with Lidia, Marco and Lolly for California. Our first goal was Detroit where I had an exhibition scheduled at the Associated Gallery of Art. Food, gas, lodging cost us over $40.00 the first day, far in excess of my optimistic estimates. We took stock of our finances and realized that at that rate we would never make Los Angeles. Lidia bought some kitchen utensils, a pressure cooker, electric plate. For the rest of the trip, we never ate in a restaurant. We found second-class hotels—just as clean and much cheaper—and there were many beautiful State camps where lodging was inexpensive and cooking facilities were provided.

I held my exhibition in Detroit, sold well there and was invited to show at the home of Mr. and Mrs. Charles Lee in Minneapolis. I flew up to Minneapolis with a group of small oils, had a successful showing there and rejoined Lidia and the children in Detroit, and we were off to Chicago.

Lidia was conducting school in the back of the car. Every morning Lolly and Marco would get their lessons in reading, writing, and arithmetic. They learned to read by reading the road signs: STOP, GO, SLOW, 30 MPH, DETOUR, ONE WAY, and the names of the towns and cities we drove through. Their mathematics consisted of checking the gasoline purchases and counting change. There were museums to visit, historic sights, and while they were out sight-seeing I stayed behind painting for an exhibition in Chicago.

Marilew Kogan and Helen Douglas Klein, old friends from the *Britannica* days, reserved a suite of rooms with kitchenette in the North Park Hotel in Chicago. I had money now and didn't have to nurse nickels. They invited the guests and, a week after we arrived in Chicago, we had an exhibition in our apartment. It was very successful thanks to Marilew, Helen, and their friends. Mr. and Mrs. Joseph Antonow bought a small painting and invited me to their beautiful home. It was a triplex apartment and had the largest living room I had ever seen. Mr. Antonow wanted to know if I could paint something for their wall, I suggested a triptych. The room had a Gothic feeling and besides I had wanted to do a triptych ever since I had been in Paris. I told him that I would dream something up on the way to the coast, paint it there and ship it back to him, but before I did, I would send him some sketches to scale for his approval. This was satisfactory to him.

We left Chicago much richer than we started. We meandered along now. No exhibitions. We stopped where we pleased for as long as we pleased. A new world opened to us as we drove into the West. We visited the Zuni Indian Reservation and spent a week at the Grand Canyon. We ambled along the Pacific from San Diego to Malibu and there found a room in a little hotel overlooking the ocean. After a few days rest we called Bob Bigelow. He thought we had perished in the desert and was about to send a posse to look for us. He introduced me to a group of young California artists. Arnold Mesches, Morty Dimondstein and Marty Lubner. They offered me the use of one of their studios for my stay. I accepted. Several days later Lidia found an apartment with Alice and Jack Thomas, lovely kind people who mothered us and whom we loved. I moved into the studio with Mesches and started to work on the triptych.

One morning just after leaving St. Louis, Lidia was singing with the children; it was a simple nursery song called "Apple Tree, Apple Tree, Drop a Ripe One Down to Me". As soon as I heard the song I had my painting for Mr. Antonow. That night I roughed it out in my sketch book. I called it *Apple Tree, Apple Tree* (page 63). I made some sketches to scale, sent them to Mr. Antonow. He sent his approval, and I went to work. It took me the seven months we were there to complete it. I was then ready to go home. I had it framed, and crated, and left it with the framer with instructions to have it shipped to coincide with my arrival in Chicago. It was my most ambitious work to date.

We took the northerly route home, spent a month in San Francisco, which gave the children a chance to attend a Chinese day school and in turn gave Lidia and me the opportunity to enjoy that wonderful city San Francisco. Near the Great Lakes I checked with Mr. Antonow and learned the painting had arrived in Chicago. I left Lidia and flew to Chicago. The Antonow family greeted me, they invited several guests, and I uncrated the painting. I set it in the middle of the immense room, opened it, closed it, and opened it, and after a few minutes of silence, they all expressed their approval. Antonow had given me carte blanche. I did not want him disappointed. He deserved to be satisfied, and he was. In 1959, after Mrs. Antonow's tragic death, he gave the triptych to Marquette University, Milwaukee, Wisconsin. Dr. John Pick, Chairman of the Marquette University Art Committee, wrote to me, telling me how happy they were to acquire the triptych and included clippings from the Milwaukee newspapers which told the whole story. He asked me to give him details of how it was painted, the story behind the painting and the title. I did. He subsequently wrote that the triptych had been installed in the Teatro Maria at Marquette University and that my letter had been framed and placed alongside the painting. We arrived home, September, 1956, one year after we had left.

I came back to New York to find that the Associated American Artists had gone out of business. For the first time in 15 years I had no New York gallery. With few exceptions, the galleries were concentrating on abstract art. Besides I didn't feel like going from gallery to gallery peddling my wares. I would wait until I was asked. I waited. Nobody asked. Galleries outside the city handled my work. Gil Golde in Great Neck was first. Donald and Florence Morris invited me to join their new gallery in Detroit. The Galerie de Ville, Beverly Hills, California, invited me to join them, and I have had several exhibitions there. Not having had a New York showing, I was anxious to have some critical evaluation of my new work. I continued to send to every important jury exhibition. My work was accepted by every jury I sent to, the last being in the 1962 Pennsylvania Academy Exhibition.

In 1958 I had an opportunity to again work on a large scale. Mr. and Mrs. Norman E. Blankman commissioned a mural for the *Sands Point Wild Life Preserve* (page 77) at Sands Point, New York. In 1962 the White Winrock Hotel of Albuquerque commissioned a series of prints for their newly-constructed hotel. I did a series of 12 subjects, and 120 prints were purchased, one for each room of the hotel.

The call to join a New York gallery finally came. Late in 1962, Sidney Bergen invited me to join the A.C.A. Gallery in New York and set January 27 to February 15, 1964 as the date for my one-man exhibition. In November, 1963, the Waldemar Medical Research Foundation commissioned me to execute a mural for their new Cancer Research and Prevention Center at Woodbury, Long Island, to be called *The Seven Ages of Man*.

Busy, busy, busy—we are all busy. Lidia has been teaching at the Friends Academy for the past five years. In her spare time she gave birth to our third child, Anna Ludmila. She is four years old and a marvelous tonic and rejuvenator for an old man of 63 looking for new doors to open.

I used to go to New York to see my friends, talk art, gossip a bit. But I gave up. I would rather go down to Louie's bar and talk to my friends there: We talk of important things —wives, dames, mortgages, fishing, children, and the shrinking size of the beer glass.

I like to think that my decision to drop the law overboard completely, or as completely as one can drop 20 years of a life, was as easy as jumping off a log. But the truth is, I was pushed. Life itself gave me a healthy nudge. My wife, Leah, had died; I was alone. I had critical acclaim, some important prizes, respected sponsorship, museum purchases, a New York gallery. And then I met and married Lidia Brestovan. She wouldn't let me equivocate. In answer to my doubts she had said, "You are a painter. Paint."

To list all the people who had helped and encouraged me is impossible—the list is too long. A special salute, however, to some who were especially kind and helpful: Mildred Constantine, Pegeen Sullivan, Herman and Ella Baron, Alfredo Valente; all the artists at the American Art School; and my teachers: Alex Dobkin who introduced me to the world of art; Sol Wilson, who, among other things, showed me that there were jewels hidden in tubes of paint; Yasuo Kuniyoshi who told me that art schools never make artists. Life sometimes does.

PLATES

ABSTRACTIONISTS, 1941

Oil on canvas

24 x 30

32   *Mr. John O'Connor Jr., Pittsburgh, Pennsylvania*

SIESTA, 1942
Oil on masonite
30 x 18
34   *The Joseph H. Hirshhorn Collection, New York*

BACK STREET, 1942
Oil on canvas
30 x 40
36 *Collection of the Metropolitan Museum of Art, Arthur H. Hearn Fund*

LUNCH, 1943
Oil
16 x 12
38   Mr. and Mrs. Dale O'Brien, Evanston, Illinois

FRIDAY FISH, 1944
Oil on canvas
24 x 34

Mr. and Mrs. Mischa Kallis, Sherman Oaks, California

BRAVADOES, 1944
Oil on masonite
24 X 12

Senator and Mrs. William Benton, Southport, Connecticut

FAMILY PORTRAIT, 1944
Oil
14 X 10
44   *Mr. and Mrs. Alfred Hitchcock, Bel Air, California*

DAY'S END, 1947
Oil on canvas
20 x 30

Mr. and Mrs. Francis Dekoven, Highland Park, Illinois

BIRDS GOTTA FLY, 1947
Oil on canvas
30 X 24

48 *The Sackler Collections, New York*

MOON OVER BLEECKER STREET, 1948
Oil
27 x 17

50 *Mr. and Mrs. Noah Jacobs, Lake Success, New York*

SPRING IS IN THE AIR, 1948
Oil on canvas
24 X 20
The Brooklyn Museum

52

BETWEEN TWO WORLDS, 1949
Oil on canvas
56 x 27
54   *Mr. and Mrs. Gerald M. Konecky, Sands Point, New York*

PIGALLE, 1950
Oil on canvas
30 x 50
A.C.A. Gallery, New York

56

KEEP OFF THE GRASS, 1951
Oil on canvas
32 X 24
A.C.A. Gallery, New York

MARCO AS INDIAN CHIEF, 1954
Oil on masonite
30 X 19
60   *A.C.A. Gallery, New York*

RAINY DAY, 1953
Oil
22 x 16
62   *Mr. Edward G. Blonder, Chicago*

APPLETREE, APPLETREE, 1956
Oil on masonite
Triptych closed, 82 x 54; Triptych open, 82 x 110
Marquette University Art Collection, Milwaukee, Wisconsin

63

BOY AND BIRD, 1956
Pastel
Mr. and Mrs. Barrows Dunham, Bala-Cynwyd, Pennsylvania

MEET MISS SUBWAYS, 1956
Oil on canvas
36 x 30
70   *A.C.A. Gallery, New York*

MRS. SMITH'S CHERRY TREE, 1957
Oil on canvas
30 x 18

Mr. and Mrs. Lester Doniger, Kenilworth, New York

AUTUMN LEAVES, 1958
Oil on canvas
32 x 25½
A.C.A. Gallery, New York

74

LISA, 1962
Oil on masonite
30 x 20

Eleanor Lenke, Port Washington, New York

COME, LET US LIGHT THE MENORAH, NO. 1, 1960
Oil on canvas
34 X 24
78 *A.C.A. Gallery, New York*

TELL ME THAT YOU LOVE ME, 1962
Oil on canvas
25½ x 21½
A.C.A. Gallery, New York

86

THE MOON IS CAUGHT IN THE TREES, 1963
Oil on canvas
30 x 20
A.C.A. Gallery, New York **87**

THIS IS THE OCEAN, 1961
Oil on masonite
11¾ x 24

88   *Mr. and Mrs. Herbert Grosberg, Detroit, Michigan*

FORBIDDEN FRUIT, 1963
Oil on masonite
24 X 52
A.C.A. Gallery, New York

90

Mr. and Mrs. José Ferrer, N.Y.C.; Mr. Paddy Chayefsky, N.Y.C.; Mr. and Mrs. Albert Mitchell, N.Y.C.; Mr. and Mrs. I. Lesser, N.Y.C.; Mr. and Mrs. R. Bettleheim, New City, N.Y.; Dr. and Mrs. Leonard Burness, N.Y.C.; Mr. and Mrs. Sam Shain, N.Y.C.; Mr. and Mrs. A. Eugene Wells, N.Y.C.; Frances Goodrich and Albert Hackett, Bel Air, Cal.; Mr. Albert Dorne, N.Y.C.; Mr. and Mrs. Edwin Eisendrath, Chicago, Ill.; Dr. and Mrs. H. M. Sperota, Chicago, Ill.; Mr. and Mrs. Herman Kogan, Chicago, Ill.; Mr. and Mrs. Edward Weiss, Chicago, Ill.; Mr. and Mrs. Marvin Mann, Chicago, Ill.; Mr. and Mrs. Walter Yust, Chicago, Ill.; Mr. and Mrs. Michael Gordon, Los Angeles, Cal.; Mr. and Mrs. B. Rabinovitch, Los Angeles, Cal.; Mr. and Mrs. Arnold Nelson, Los Angeles, Cal.; Mr. Leonard Spigelgass, Los Angeles, Cal.; Mr. Joseph Heller, N.Y.C.; Mr. and Mrs. Norman Blankman, Sands Point, N.Y.; Mr. and Mrs. Alfredo Valente, Glen Cove, N.Y.; Miss Vivian Rifkin, N.Y.C.; Mr. and Mrs. M. K. Breslauer, N.Y.C.; Mr. and Mrs. S. Edelberg, Jackson Heights, N.Y.; Mr. and Mrs. Leon Bernstein, Great Neck, N.Y.; Mr. and Mrs. David Bady, N.Y.C.; Mr. and Mrs. C. A. Bristel, Great Neck, N.Y.; Mr. and Mrs. M. Aronstein, Great Neck, N.Y.; Mr. and Mrs. Morris Kinzler, N.Y.C.; Mr. and Mrs. Samuel Aronowitz, Great Neck, N.Y.; Mr. and Mrs. M. Zaid, Plainview, N.Y.; Mr. and Mrs. M. S. Sharaga, Plainview, N.Y.; Mr. and Mrs. William Stieglitz, Forest Hills, N.Y.; Mr. and Mrs. A. Novak, Brooklyn, N.Y.; Mr. and Mrs. N. Shields, Rockville Centre, N.Y.; Mr. and Mrs. Herman Abramson, Rockville Centre, N.Y.; Mr. and Mrs. M. Finkelstein, Great Neck, N.Y.; Mr. and Mrs. Saul Victor, Irvington, N.Y.; Mr. and Mrs. Robert Friedlander, Interlaken, N. J.; Mr. and Mrs. H. A. Becher, Rockville Centre, N.Y.; Mr. and Mrs. Robert Polon, Rockville Centre, N.Y.; Mr. and Mrs. L. Abrams, N.Y.C.; Mr. and Mrs. Harry Ackerman, Los Angeles, Cal.; Mr. and Mrs. A. Aibel, Roslyn Heights, N.Y.; Mr. and Mrs. Marvin Bruck, Westport, Conn.; Mr. and Mrs. Joby Baker, Los Angeles, Cal.; Dr. and Mrs. Harold Blank, Great Neck, N.Y.; Mr. and Mrs. R. Brooks, Great Neck, N.Y.; Mr. and Mrs. S. W. Cantor, Great Neck, N.Y.; Mr. and Mrs.. M. Chaiken, Great Neck, N.Y.; Mr. and Mrs. L. R. Cohn, Manhasset, N.Y.; Mr. and Mrs. William Cone, Great Neck, N.Y.; Mr. and Mrs. Gordon Crowe, Mamaroneck, N.Y.; Mr. and Mrs. S. L. Dewey, Huntington, N.Y.; Mr. and Mrs. Alfred Eliot, Great Neck, N.Y.; Mr. and Mrs. I. Fabrikant, N.Y.C.; Mr. and Mrs. C. Feller, Plainview, N.Y.; Mr. and Mrs. Joseph Fine, Great Neck, N.Y.; Mr. and Mrs. Carl Frank, Garden City, N.Y.; Dr. and Mrs. H. L. Green,

Great Neck, N.Y.; Mr. and Mrs. Allen Harvey, Scarsdale, N.Y.; Mr. and Mrs. Zola Harvey, Great Neck, N.Y.; Mr. and Mrs. Norman Stern, Great Neck, N.Y.; Louis Held Collection, N.Y.C.; Mr. and Mrs. H. Holtzman, Roslyn Heights, N.Y.; Mr. and Mrs. F. H. Iger, Sands Point, N.Y. Mr. and Mrs. Saul Jaffee, N.Y.C.; Mr. and Mrs. F. Jaroslow, Manhasset, N.Y.; Mr. and Mrs. Lou Kaplan, Great Neck, N.Y.; Mr. and Mrs. Murray Kaplan, Great Neck, N.Y.; Mr. and Mrs. Ray Kellman, East Norwich, N.Y.; Dr. and Mrs. B. Kissin, Brooklyn, N.Y.; Mr. and Mrs. E. Klaven, Great Neck, N.Y.; Mr. and Mrs. Mortimer Levine, Great Neck, N.Y.; Mr. and Mrs. Sidney Kleinman, Great Neck, N.Y.; Mr. and Mrs. Dan Krackauer, Great Neck, N.Y.; Dr. and Mrs. B. Kronenberg, N.Y.C.; Mr. and Mrs. Robert Krumholz, Brooklyn, N.Y.; Dr. Gail Borden, Port Washington, N.Y.; Dr. and Mrs. Leroy Lavine, Great Neck, N.Y.; Mr. and Mrs. Richard Lawrence, Kings Point, N.Y.; Mr. and Mrs. Justice Joseph Liff, Great Neck, N.Y.; Mr. and Mrs. Harry Lowe, N.Y.C.; Mr. and Mrs. Milton Lowenthal, N.Y.C.; Mr. and Mrs. Harold Meyers, Mamaroneck, N.Y.; Mr. and Mrs. George Wittner, N.Y.C.; Mr. and Mrs. Lawrence Meyers, N.Y.C.; Mr. and Mrs. M. Nebenzahl, Kings Point, N.Y.; Mr. and Mrs. Ralph C. Raughley, Great Neck, N.Y.; Mr. and Mrs. John Rapp, Los Angeles, Cal.; Dr. and Mrs. Bernard A. Roberts, Maplewood, N.J.; Mr. and Mrs. Murray Roth, N.Y.C.; Mr. and Mrs. Herman Wechsler, N.Y.C.; Mr. and Mrs. Stanley Sadkin, Newark, N.J.; Dr. and Mrs. A. Salzberg, Great Neck, N.Y.; Mr. and Mrs. L. H. Sleppin, N.Y.C.; Mr. and Mrs. Lionel Sokolov, Sands Point, N.Y.; Dr. and Mrs. I. Stern, Forest Hills, N.Y.; Mr. and Mrs. Howard Swift, Manorhaven, N.Y.; Mrs. Florence Lazare, Freeport, N.Y.; Dr. and Mrs. Jack M. Topal, Forest Hills, N.Y.; Mr. and Mrs. M. Uris, N.Y.C.; Mr. and Mrs. Alfred Van Loen, Huntington, N.Y.; Mr. and Mrs. Sidney Wasserman, N.Y.C.; Dr. and Mrs. Geza Weitzner, N.Y.C.; Mr. and Mrs. J. Friedman, Great Neck, N.Y.; Mr. and Mrs. William Landsberg, Port Washington, N.Y.; Mr. and Mrs. H. Levy, Great Neck, N.Y.; Dr. and Mrs. S. Langer, Great Neck, N.Y.; Mr. and Mrs. Harold Mertz, Sands Point, N.Y.; Mr. and Mrs. Irving Lefcourt, N.Y.C.; Mr. and Mrs. Samuel Paul, Hewlett, N.Y.; Mr. and Mrs. Bernard Rappaport, Great Neck, N.Y.; Mr. and Mrs. S. W. Kantor, Great Neck, N.Y.; Mr. and Mrs. Louis B. Rappaport, Sands Point, N.Y.; Mr. and Mrs. Alfred Hagedorn, Jr., Sands Point, N.Y.; Mr. and Mrs. Aaron M. Scharf, Sands Point, N.Y.

Paintings

The Abbott Collection, Chicago, Illinois

Auburn University, Auburn, Alabama

Brandeis University, Waltham, Massachusetts

Fine Arts Museum, Moscow, U.S.S.R.

Marquette University, Milwaukee, Wisconsin

Sewanhaka High School, Floral Park, N.Y.

The Brooklyn Museum, Brooklyn, N.Y.

The Metropolitan Museum of Art, New York

The Encyclopaedia Britannica Collection,
    Chicago, Illinois

The University of Oklahoma, Norman,
    Oklahoma

The Tel Aviv Museum, Tel Aviv, Israel

The Phillips Gallery, Washington, D.C.

The Newark Museum, Newark, New Jersey

The University of Arizona, Tucson, Arizona

Prints

Syracuse University, Syracuse, New York

Port Washington Public Library,
    Port Washington, New York

Main Street School, Port Washington, New York

North Shore Hospital, Manhasset, New York

Murals

1958: Sands Point Wild Life Preserve, Sands
        Point, New York

1964: Waldemar Cancer Research and Preven-
        tion Center, Woodbury, New York

AWARDS AND HONORS

1942: Artists for Victory, The Metropolitan
        Museum of Art: $500 Purchase Prize

1943: Invitation Exhibition, The Phillips
        Gallery

1952: Traveling Exhibition, sponsored by the
        American Federation of Arts

1953: First Prize for Painting, Manhasset Art
        Annual

Design: MICHAEL B. ROLSTON

Typographic Composition: HUXLEY HOUSE, LTD., New York City
Display type, *Optima*
Text type, *Linotype Baskerville*

Printing: SHOREWOOD PRESS, Plainview, New York
Paper, *Andorra Text*—Hamilton Paper Co.

Binding: J. F. TAPLEY COMPANY, Long Island City, New York
End papers, *Mi-Teintes*—Canson & Montgolfier, France
Binding cloth, *Bradford Linen*—Columbia Mills

Photography: *For Duotone Reproductions*—John Ebstel, S. Colten, Sanford Goldrich
For Color Reproductions—Shorewood Press